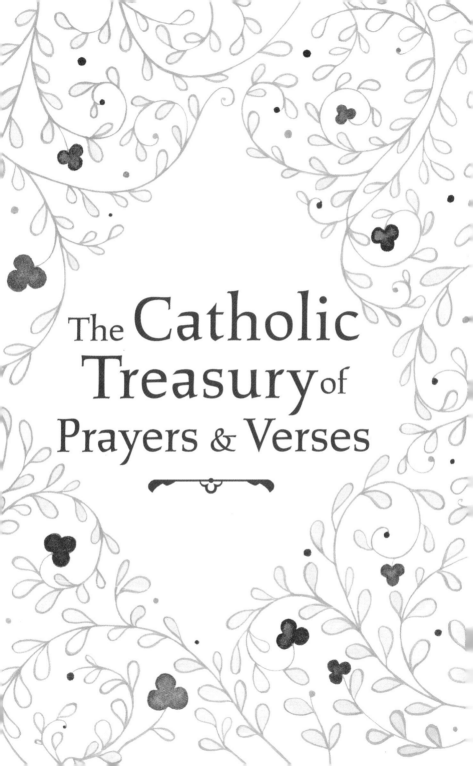

The Catholic Treasury of Prayers & Verses

able of Contents

Sacred Scripture

he Divine Shepherd

Psalm 23

The LORD is my shepherd, I shall not want;
he makes me lie down in green pastures.
He leads me beside still waters;
he restores my soul.
He leads me in paths of righteousness
for his name's sake.

Even though I walk through the valley of the
shadow of death,
I fear no evil;
for you are with me;
your rod and your staff,
they comfort me.

You prepare a table before me
in the presence of my enemies;
you anoint my head with oil,
my cup overflows.

Surely goodness and mercy shall follow me
all the days of my life;
and I shall dwell in the house of the LORD
for ever.

A Word of Everlasting Praise
Psalm 106:1

Praise the LORD!
O give thanks to the LORD, for he is good;
for his steadfast love endures for ever!

The Duty of God's Children
Micah 6:8

He has showed you, O man, what is good;
and what does the LORD require of you
but to do justice, and to love kindness,
and to walk humbly with your God?

The Fruits of the Spirit
Galatians 5:22-23

The fruit of the Spirit is love, joy, peace, patience,
kindness, goodness, faithfulness, gentleness,
and self-control.

The Magnificat

Luke 1:46-55

My soul magnifies the Lord,
and my spirit rejoices in God my Savior,
for he has regarded the low estate of his handmaiden.

For behold, henceforth all generations will call me blessed;
for he who is mighty has done great things for me,
and holy is his name.
And his mercy is on those who fear him
from generation to generation.

He has shown strength with his arm,
he has scattered the proud in the imagination of their hearts,
he has put down the mighty from their thrones,
and exalted those of low degree;
he has filled the hungry with good things,
and the rich he has sent empty away.

He has helped his servant Israel,
in remembrance of his mercy,
as he spoke to our fathers,
to Abraham and to his posterity for ever.

The Greatest Commandment
John 13:34

new commandment I give to you,
that you love one another;
even as I have loved you,
that you also love one another.

The Gift of Love
1 Corinthians 13:4-8, 13

ove is patient and kind;
love is not jealous or boastful;
it is not arrogant or rude.
Love does not insist on its own way;
it is not irritable or resentful;
it does not rejoice at wrong,
but rejoices in the right.
Love bears all things,
believes all things,
hopes all things,
endures all things.
Love never ends.
So faith, hope, love abide, these three;
but the greatest of these is love.

The Beatitudes

Matthew 5:3-12

Blessed are the poor in spirit, for theirs is the kingdom of heaven.

Blessed are those who mourn, for they shall be comforted.

Blessed are the meek, for they shall inherit the earth.

Blessed are those who hunger and thirst for righteousness, for they shall be satisfied.

Blessed are the merciful, for they shall obtain mercy.

Blessed are the pure in heart, for they shall see God.

Blessed are the peacemakers, for they shall be called sons of God.

Blessed are those who are persecuted for righteousness' sake, for theirs is the kingdom of heaven.

Blessed are you when men revile you and persecute you and utter all kinds of evil against you falsely on my account.

Rejoice and be glad, for your reward is great in heaven, for so men persecuted the prophets who were before you.

May God's Peace Be with You
Philippians 4:8

Whatever is true, whatever is
honorable, whatever is just, whatever
is pure, whatever is lovely, whatever
is gracious, if there is any excellence,
if there is anything worthy of praise,
think about these things.

The Glory of God's Law
Psalm 119:105

Your word is a lamp to my feet, and a
light to my path.

The Great Commission

Matthew 28: 19-20

Go therefore and make disciples of all nations,
baptizing them in the name of the
Father and of the Son and of the Holy Spirit,
teaching them to observe all that I have
commanded you;
and behold, I am with you always,
to the close of the age.

A Prayer in
God's Presence
Psalm 63: 1-4

O God, you are my God, I seek you,
my soul thirsts for you;
my flesh faints for you,
as in a dry and weary land where
no water is.

So I have looked upon you in the
sanctuary, beholding your power
and glory.
Because your merciful love is
better than life,
my lips will praise you.

So I will bless you as long as I live;
I will lift up my hands and call on
your name.

Catholic Prayers

The Lord's Prayer

Our Father,
Who art in Heaven, hallowed be Thy name;
Thy Kingdom come,
Thy will be done on earth as it is in Heaven.

Give us this day our daily bread;
and forgive us our trespasses as we forgive those
who trespass against us;
and lead us not into temptation,
but deliver us from evil. Amen.

Hail Mary

Hail Mary, full of Grace,
the Lord is with thee.
Blessed art thou among women and blessed
is the fruit of thy womb, Jesus.

Holy Mary, Mother of God,
pray for us sinners, now and at the
hour of our death. Amen.

Glory Be

Glory be to the Father and to the Son
and to the Holy Spirit,
as it was in the beginning, is now,
and ever shall be,
world without end. Amen.

The Apostles' Creed

I believe in God,
the Father almighty,
Creator of heaven and earth,
and in Jesus Christ, his only Son, our Lord,
who was conceived by the Holy Spirit,
born of the Virgin Mary,
suffered under Pontius Pilate,
was crucified, died and was buried;
he descended into hell;
on the third day he rose again from the dead;
he ascended into heaven,
and is seated at the right hand of God the Father almighty;
from there he will come to judge the living and the dead.

I believe in the Holy Spirit,
the holy catholic Church,
the communion of saints,
the forgiveness of sins,
the resurrection of the body,
and life everlasting. Amen.

Hail, Holy Queen

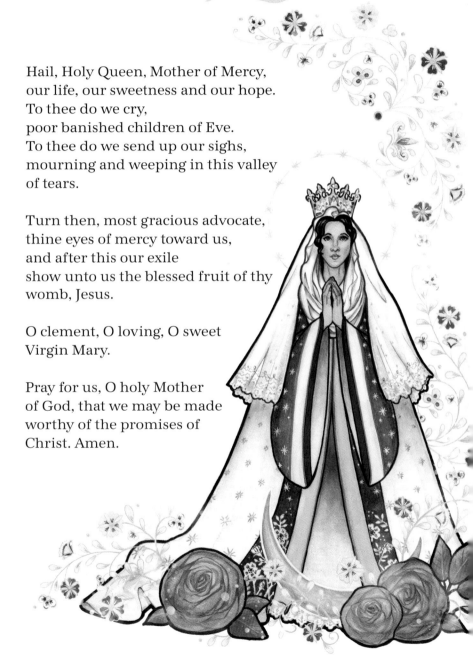

Hail, Holy Queen, Mother of Mercy,
our life, our sweetness and our hope.
To thee do we cry,
poor banished children of Eve.
To thee do we send up our sighs,
mourning and weeping in this valley
of tears.

Turn then, most gracious advocate,
thine eyes of mercy toward us,
and after this our exile
show unto us the blessed fruit of thy
womb, Jesus.

O clement, O loving, O sweet
Virgin Mary.

Pray for us, O holy Mother
of God, that we may be made
worthy of the promises of
Christ. Amen.

How to Pray the Rosary

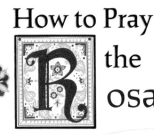

1. Make the Sign of the Cross and say the Apostles' Creed.

2. Say the Our Father.

3. Say the Hail Mary three times for Faith, Hope, and Charity.

4. Say the Glory Be.

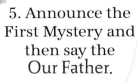

5. Announce the First Mystery and then say the Our Father.

6. Say the Hail Mary ten times while meditating on the Mystery.

7. Say the Glory Be (Optional: Say the Fatima Prayer).

8. Repeat for each Mystery.

9. Say the closing prayers: the Hail Holy Queen and Final Prayer. Conclude with the Sign of the Cross.

The Fatima Prayer

O My Jesus, forgive us our sins, save us from the fires of Hell and lead all souls to Heaven, especially those who are in most need of Thy mercy.

Final Prayer

Let us pray. O God, whose Only Begotten Son, by His life, death, and resurrection, has purchased for us the rewards of eternal life, grant, we beseech Thee, that meditating upon these mysteries of the Most Holy Rosary of the Blessed Virgin Mary, we may imitate what they contain and obtain what they promise, through the same Christ Our Lord. Amen.

The Mysteries of the Rosary

Joyful Mysteries
Pray on Monday and Saturday
- The Annunciation of the Lord to Mary
- Mary's Visitation to Her Cousin Elizabeth
- The Nativity of Our Lord Jesus Christ
- The Presentation of Our Lord Jesus Christ
- Finding Jesus in the Temple

Sorrowful Mysteries
Pray on Tuesday and Friday
- Jesus' Agony in the Garden of Gethsemane
- The Scourging at the Pillar
- Jesus is Crowned with Thorns
- Jesus Carries His Cross
- The Crucifixion and Death of Jesus

Glorious Mysteries
Pray on Wednesday and Sunday
- The Resurrection of Jesus
- The Ascension of Jesus into Heaven
- The Descent of the Holy Spirit at Pentecost
- The Assumption of Mary
- The Crowning of Mary, Queen of Heaven and Earth

Luminous Mysteries
Pray on Thursday
- Jesus' Baptism in the Jordan River
- The Wedding Feast of Cana
- The Proclamation of the Gospel
- The Transfiguration
- The Institution of the Eucharist

Morning Offering

O Jesus, through the Immaculate Heart
of Mary, I offer You my prayers, works, joys,
and sufferings of this day for all the intentions of
Your Sacred Heart, in union with the Holy
Sacrifice of the Mass throughout the world, in
reparation for my sins, for the intentions of all
my relatives and friends, and in particular for
the intentions of the Holy Father. Amen.

Guardian Angel Prayer

Angel of God, my guardian dear,
to whom His love commits me here,
Ever this day be at my side,
to light and guard, to rule and guide.
Amen.

Come, Holy Spirit

Come Holy Spirit, fill the hearts of Your faithful and kindle in them the fire of Your love. Send forth Your Spirit and they shall be created. And You shall renew the face of the earth.

O, God, who by the light of the Holy Spirit, did instruct the hearts of the faithful, grant that by the same Holy Spirit we may be truly wise and ever enjoy His consolations, Through Christ Our Lord, Amen.

Prayer to the Sacred Heart of Jesus

May the Sacred Heart of Jesus
be adored, glorified, loved
and preserved throughout the
world, now and forever.

Sacred Heart of Jesus, have
mercy on us. Amen.

Memorare

Remember,
O most gracious Virgin Mary,
that never was it known that
anyone who fled to your protection,
implored your help, or sought your
intercession, was left unaided.
Inspired by this confidence,
I fly unto you, O Virgin of
virgins, my Mother.

To you do I come, before you I
stand, sinful and sorrowful.

O Mother of the Word Incarnate,
despise not my petitions,
but in your mercy hear and
answer me. Amen.

St. Michael Prayer

St. Michael the Archangel, defend us in battle,
be our protection against the wickedness
and snares of the devil.
May God rebuke him, we humbly pray;
and do thou, O Prince of the heavenly host,
by the power of God, cast into hell Satan
and all the evil spirits who prowl about the
world seeking the ruin of souls.
Amen.

The Divine Praises

Blessed be God.
Blessed be His Holy Name.
Blessed be Jesus Christ, true God and true Man.
Blessed be the Name of Jesus.
Blessed be His Most Sacred Heart.
Blessed be His Most Precious Blood.
Blessed be Jesus in the Most Holy Sacrament of the Altar.
Blessed be the Holy Spirit, the Paraclete.
Blessed be the great Mother of God, Mary most Holy.
Blessed be her Holy and Immaculate Conception.
Blessed be her Glorious Assumption.
Blessed be the name of Mary, Virgin and Mother.
Blessed be St. Joseph, her most chaste spouse.
Blessed be God in His Angels and in His Saints.
Amen.

Act of Contrition

My God, I am sorry for my sins with all my heart.
In choosing to do wrong and failing to do good,
I have sinned against You whom I should love above all things.

I firmly intend, with Your help, to do penance, to sin no more, and to avoid whatever leads me to sin.
Our Savior Jesus Christ suffered and died for us.
In His name, my God, have mercy.

Eucharistic Prayers

 nima Christi

A Prayer by St. Ignatius of Loyola

Soul of Christ, sanctify me.
Body of Christ, save me.
Blood of Christ, inebriate me.
Water from the side of Christ, wash me.
Passion of Christ, strengthen me.
O good Jesus, hear me.
Within Your wounds hide me.
Let me never be separated from You.
From the malignant enemy, defend me.
At the hour of death, call me.
And bid me to come to you,
That with Your saints I may praise You,
forever and ever. Amen.

Act of Spiritual Communion

A Prayer by St. Alphonsus Ligouri

My Jesus,
I believe that You are present in the
Most Holy Sacrament.
I love You above all things,
and I desire to receive You into my soul.
Since I cannot at this moment receive
You sacramentally,
come at least spiritually into my heart.
I embrace You as if You were already there
and unite myself wholly to You.
Never permit me to be separated from You. Amen.

Prayer

Before Receiving Communion

A Prayer by St. Thomas Aquinas

Grant unto me, I pray, the grace of receiving not only the Sacrament of our Lord's Body and Blood, but also the grace and power of the Sacrament.

O most gracious God, grant me so to receive the Body of Your only-begotten Son, Our Lord Jesus Christ, which He took from the Virgin Mary, as to merit to be drawn into His mystical Body, and to be numbered among His members.

O most loving Father, give me grace to behold forever Your beloved Son with His face at last unveiled, whom I now receive under the sacramental veil here below. Amen.

Prayer After Receiving Communion

A Prayer by St. Padre Pio

Stay with me, Lord, to show me Your will.

Stay with me, Lord, so that I hear Your voice and follow You.

Stay with me, Lord, for I desire to love You very much and always be in Your company.

Stay with me, Lord, if You wish me to be faithful to You.

Stay with me, Lord, as poor as my soul is, I want it to be a place of consolation for You, a nest of love. Amen.

Prayer

Before the Tabernacle

A Prayer by St. Francis of Assisi

We adore You,
O Lord Jesus Christ,
in this church and all the churches of the world
and we bless You, because,
by Your holy Cross
You have redeemed the world.

Saint
Prayers

Prayer to St. Joseph

O St. Joseph, whose protection is so great, so strong,
so prompt before the throne of God,
I place in you all my interests and desires.

O St. Joseph, assist me by your powerful intercession
and obtain for me all spiritual blessings through your
foster Son, Jesus Christ Our Lord, so that,
having shown here below your heavenly power,
I may offer you my thanksgiving and homage.

O St. Joseph, I never weary contemplating you
and Jesus asleep in your arms.
I dare not approach while He rests near your heart.
Press Him in my name and kiss His fine head for me,
and ask Him to return the kiss
when I draw my dying breath.

St. Joseph, patron of departing souls, pray for me.

Amen.

St. Thérèse's Prayer to the Child Jesus

O Jesus, dear Holy Child, my only treasure,
I abandon myself to Your every whim.
I seek no other joy than that of calling forth
Your sweet Smile.

Give me the graces and the virtues of Your
Holy Childhood,
so that on the day of my birth into
Heaven the Angels and Saints
may recognize me as Your
Spouse. Amen.

St. Clement's Prayer for All Needs

We beg You, Lord,
to help and defend us.
Deliver the oppressed,
pity the insignificant,
raise the fallen,
show yourself to the needy,
heal the sick,
bring back those of your people who
have gone astray,
feed the hungry,
lift up the weak,
take off the prisoners' chains.

May every nation come to know
that you alone are God,
that Jesus Christ is your Child,
that we are your people, the sheep that
you pasture. Amen.

Prayer of
St. John Henry Newman

Dear Jesus, help me to spread Your fragrance
everywhere I go.

Flood my soul with Your spirit and life.

Penetrate and possess my whole being so utterly,
That my life may only be a radiance of Yours.

Shine through me, and be so in me
That every soul I come in contact with
May feel Your presence in my soul.

Let them look up and see no longer me,
but only Jesus! Amen.

Prayer of St. Benedict

O Lord, I place myself in Your hands and dedicate myself to You.
I pledge myself to do Your will in all things:
To love the Lord God with all my heart, all my soul, all my strength.
Not to kill. Not to steal. Not to covet.
Not to bear false witness.
To honor all persons. Not to do to another what I would not wish done to myself.
To remember that God sees me everywhere.
To call upon Christ for defense against evil thoughts that arise in my heart.
To guard my tongue against wicked speech.
To avoid much speaking. To avoid idle talk.
To read only what is good to read. To look at only what is good to see.
To pray often.
To ask forgiveness daily for my sins, and to seek ways to amend my life.
To pray for my enemies.
To make peace after a quarrel, before the setting of the sun.
Never to despair of your mercy, O God of Mercy.
Amen.

rayer of

St. Teresa Benedicta of the Cross

O Prince of Peace,
to all who receive You,
You bright light and peace.

Help me to live in daily contact with You,
listening to the words You have spoken
and obeying them.

O Divine Child, I place my hands in Yours;
I shall follow You. Let Your divine life flow
into me. Amen.

St. Ignatius of Loyola's Prayer for the Dead

Lord, welcome into Your calm and peaceful
kingdom those who have departed out of this
present life to be with you.

Grant them rest and a place with the spirits of the
just; and give them the life that shows no age,
the reward that passes not away,
through Christ Our Lord.

Amen.

St. Teresa of Calcutta's

Prayer for Every Day

Give us a heart as beautiful, pure, and spotless as Yours. A heart like Yours, so full of love and humility.

May we be able to receive Jesus as the Bread of Life, to love Him as You loved Him, to serve Him under the mistreated face of the poor.

We ask this through Jesus Christ Our Lord. Amen.

Prayer to
My Patron Saint

My dear patron saint,
I ask you to intercede before the
throne of God for me.
Pray that my faith may increase.
Ask for the grace I need to be holy.
Guard me against sin.
Lead me along the path to heaven so
that, one day, I may rejoice with you in
the presence of my Father in heaven.
Amen.

Litany of Saints

Lord, have mercy on us.
Christ, have mercy on us.
Lord, have mercy on us.
Christ, hear us.
Christ, graciously hear us.
God, the Father of Heaven, have mercy on us.
God, the Son, Redeemer of the world,
have mercy on us.
God, the Holy Spirit, have mercy on us.
Holy Trinity, one God, pray for us.
Holy Virgin of virgins, pray for us.
St. Michael, pray for us.
St. Gabriel, pray for us.
St. Raphael, pray for us.
All you Holy Angels and Archangels, pray for us.
St. John the Baptist, pray for us.
St. Joseph, pray for us.
All you Holy Patriarchs and Prophets, pray for us.
All you Holy Apostles and Evangelists, pray for us.
All you Holy Disciples of the Lord, pray for us.
All you Holy Innocents, pray for us.
(Add your personal patrons and favorite saints) . . .
pray for us.
All you Holy Men and Women, Pray for us.
Amen.

We
Believe

# The Ten Commandments

1. I am the LORD your God: You shall not have strange Gods before me.

2. You shall not take the name of the LORD your God in vain.

3. Remember to keep holy the LORD's Day.

4. Honor your father and mother.

5. You shall not kill.

6. You shall not commit adultery.

7. You shall not steal.

8. You shall not bear false witness against your neighbor.

9. You shall not covet your neighbor's wife.

10. You shall not covet your neighbor's goods.

Spiritual Works of Mercy

Counsel the doubtful
Instruct the ignorant
Admonish the sinner
Comfort the sorrowful
Forgive injuries
Bear wrongs patiently
Pray for the living and the dead

Corporal Works of Mercy

Feed the hungry
Give drink to the thirsty
Shelter the homeless
Visit the sick
Visit the imprisoned
Bury the dead
Give alms to the poor

The Seven Sacraments

Baptism

Eucharist

Confirmation

Reconciliation

Anointing of the Sick

Marriage

Holy Orders

The Three Theological Virtues

Faith: We believe in God and all He has revealed.

Hope: We trust in Christ's promise that eternal life is our ultimate happiness.

Love, or Charity: We love God above all, and we love our neighbors as ourselves, out of love for God.

The Four Cardinal Virtues

Prudence: The virtue that helps us know what is good and to choose the right way to achieve that good.

Justice: The virtue that guides us to give God and others what they are due.

Fortitude: The virtue that strengthens us to remain faithful in pursuing what is good.

Temperance: The virtue that keeps our desire for pleasures and other goods in balance.

Emmaus Road Publishing
1468 Parkview Circle
Steubenville, Ohio 43952

Illustrations ©2020 Adalee Hude
All rights reserved. Published 2020
Printed in the United States of America

Library of Congress Control Number: 2020944397
ISBN 978-1-64585-066-3 hardcover | 978-1-64585-067-0 ebook

Cover design and layout by Emily Demary